Cosby

by
Dennis P. Eichhorn

A *Reading Success* Paperback Book

Turman Publishing Company
Seattle

Author: Dennis P. Eichhorn

Series Editor: Louise Morgan

Photo Credits: ABC; CBS; Cleveland Press Historical Library; Richard Meek—p.56; NBC; Warner Bros.

Harris-Jacobson Rating 4

An Unauthorized Biography

Copyright © 1986 Turman Publishing Company
1319 Dexter Avenue North
Seattle, Washington 98109

Catalog No. 200
Library of Congress Catalog Card Number: 88-50801
ISBN 0-89872-200-4
Printed in the United States of America.

CONTENTS

NOTE: A glossary of unfamiliar terms is provided at the end of each chapter.

The most popular family in the history of American television—The Huxtables, starring Bill Cosby.

CHAPTER 1

He's Done It All

Bill Cosby is a man with a quiet mission. He wants to change things for the better. Bill knows that his work can be inspirational to others. He came up the hard way and made plenty of mistakes. Now, he wants to help young people avoid making those same mistakes. "I believe in learning from your mistakes and not becoming bitter," Bill says. "Unhappiness should make a person appreciate happiness more, and hard times should give a person backbone and moral strength."

Coming from a single-parent home, Bill appreciates a family. He believes that he is most successful as a husband and father. Bill's latest hit TV series, *The Cosby Show,* has given him the chance to play the part of Dr. Cliff Huxtable, a character who is much like the real Bill Cosby. The world has looked into Bill Cosby's heart through the medium of TV, and people everywhere like what they've seen. Bill Cosby has become a father figure to millions of viewers around the globe.

Bill believes in education. He found out the hard way, dropping out of both high school and college, and then going back and trying harder than ever to learn what he needed to know. Bill learned early in life that he could entertain people and make them laugh, and he's developed that talent in many directions, establishing himself in every corner of the entertainment world.

Starting out as an unknown stand-up comic on the East Coast, Bill's career blossomed almost overnight. Now, Bill Cosby may be considered the most popular entertainer in the world. Millions of people trust and admire him. Performing as a comedian, actor, and musician since the 1960s, he's recorded more than two dozen albums of comedy and music, acted in five TV series and ten movies, and made thousands of stage appearances as a stand-up comedian. Bill has continued to grow more popular every year.

Bill's first six comedy albums each won Grammy Awards as Best Comedy Album of the year. His first TV series, *I Spy,* was a big success, and Bill won the Emmy Award for Best Actor in a dramatic TV series three years in a row.

And there have been ads. Bill has been in commercials for Ford, Texas Instruments, Del Monte, Coca-Cola, and Jell-O Pudding, to name a few. People trust Bill, and he endorses only products that he believes in. ''I'm a tremendous pitchman,'' he admits.

He's Done It All

Although Bill has been in ten films, he's never enjoyed the same recognition as a movie actor that he has as a comedian and TV actor. He isn't worried about that. "I don't care about being a movie star," he says. Bill is too busy doing other things, such as producing and writing *The Cosby Show* and working on other TV shows. Somehow, Bill found time to write a book about being a father.

Basically, Bill is just a likeable guy who stands up on stage and tells funny stories. "What I'm trying to do professionally is get people to like me," Bill says. One thing has led to another, and now Bill is a big star. "I don't consider myself a superstar," he says. "I think I'm a star who does what I do very well. I consider myself a master of stand-up comedy, and I still really enjoy performing. But, of course, I have developed. *The Cosby Show* is exactly what I enjoy doing most. I decided I wanted to do a TV show that all my children could watch without my wife and me worrying about how it would affect them. The success of the show has gone way past what I expected."

Why do people watch the show? Bill feels, "It's because of the family. When the show is over, I think people have the same reaction I have to it: I smile and feel good."

Bill's varied success can be credited to his positive outlook on life and on people. Bill doesn't waste time worrying about the past. "I don't usually look back and regret or try to figure out how things *could* have been different," he says. "I look to the future."

Glossary

This glossary gives an explanation of how certain words were used in this book. A definition of each word can be found in a dictionary.

admire   look up to.

affect   have an effect on.

appreciate   be thankful for.

avoid   keep away from.

backbone   strength to hold himself up.

basically   mainly.

believes in   feels good about.

bitter   angry.

career blossomed   his job grew.

commercials   short films that sell something.

consider   think of.

credited   owing to.

developed   made better.

directions   different ways to go.

dramatic   a show that tells a serious story.

dropping out   quitting.

education   learning.

endorses   says it is good.

entertain   delight or amuse people.

entertainer   a person who delights or amuses people.

establishing   setting.

expected   thought would happen.

father figure   picture of a good father.

figure out   find out.

globe   world.

inspirational   makes people think.

master   person who can do it well.

medium   way of.

moral strength   strength to do what you believe is right.

overnight   in a short time.

pitchman   person who speaks out for something.

positive outlook   he sees life as good.

products   things that are made.

quiet mission   personal goal in life.

reaction   what a person does after watching the show.

recognition   being famous for.

recorded   put on record.

single-parent home   one parent in the house.

superstar   one of the most popular people in show business.

talent   natural ability.

trust   believe.

varied   different.

viewers   people who watch TV.

CHAPTER **2**
Growing Up

William Henry Cosby, Jr., was born on July 12, 1937, in Germantown, a district of Philadelphia in Pennsylvania. His parents were William Cosby, Sr., a mess steward in the Navy, and Anna Cosby, a housemaid. The Cosbys lived in the Richard Allen housing project in North Philadelphia. Bill was the eldest child. His brothers are Russell and Robert. A third brother, James, died of rheumatic fever at the age of six.

Bill's father wasn't around very much. "I love my father, and he loves me, but the old man wasn't the outstanding part of my life," Bill says. "My father was an intelligent man who failed in life. When I was a child we kept moving down the economic ladder. My father left home many, many times. He would leave when the rent was due or come home penniless on payday, swearing to my mother that he'd been robbed and then leave again.

Bill revisits the Philadelphia neighborhood where he grew up.

"Once he vanished just before Christmas, and we didn't have a cent. I wanted to cheer everybody up, so I took an orange crate and painted it with water colors. We had a little Santa that lit up, and I put that on top. When my mother saw it—about 9 p.m. on Christmas Eve—she put on her coat and went out. She must have borrowed some money from the neighbors because she came back with a kind of scrawny Christmas tree, and the next morning we all had a few little presents.

"The thing I remember about being a child was being poor. I remember the eviction signs especially. They were doubly hard to take. My family was receiving welfare and public assistance, and we really needed it. Without it, we wouldn't have had clothes.

"But when you're young, you have all kinds of energy; you forget the bad things and get on with the good: playing ball, going downtown with your friends to shine shoes and sell shopping bags, making $2 and coming back home. In that neighborhood, we never had an image to look up to, aside from the minister. The people I looked up to were the guys who told good stories."

Anna Cosby raised her three sons while working long hours cleaning houses to earn money for food and rent. "She's the most unselfish person I've ever known," Bill says of his mother. "Many's the time I saw her come home from work, exhausted and hungry, and she'd give her supper to one of my brothers who was still hungry after he'd eaten his own." Bill cared what his mother thought of him. "The thing that always turned me around and kept me from taking a pistol and holding up a store was that I could go to jail, and this would bring a great amount of shame on my mother," he says.

Instead, Bill found jobs that brought in a little money for the Cosby family. "My first job was to make a shoeshine box out of orange crates," he remembers. "Then I went out and bought shoe polish and washrags and went downtown to shine shoes. When I was 11, I worked over summer vacation at a grocery store, hauling boxes and stuff from 6 in the morning until 6 at night for eight dollars a week. That was 1948. Later on, I worked at a soda fountain.''

In the fifth grade, Bill made up his first comedy routine for his classmates. His teacher found him so funny that she asked him to repeat the sketch, and Bill did. That was his first encore. Bill had discovered comedy. "I found I could make people laugh, and I enjoyed doing it," he says. "I thought that if people laughed at what I said, that meant they liked me. For me, telling funny stories became a way of making friends."

Bill began to entertain his friends with jokes and stories. He was fond of listening to his mother read stories from the Bible and by Mark Twain, and Bill learned how to spin a tale that would entertain an audience. "William is an alert boy who would rather clown than study," his sixth-grade teacher wrote on his report card. Bill admits this was true. "To get my thoughts across and to be an important person, I made people laugh," he says. "Through humor, I gained acceptance."

Bill began to develop as an athlete, too. He played street football and schoolyard basketball. He also learned to appreciate jazz. "When I was 11 years old, I bought my first pair of drumsticks and learned how to play drums," Bill says. "I'm a self-taught drummer. I love jazz—not the kind you snap your fingers or tap your foot to, but the kind that grabs your intestines and ties them in a knot."

The famous Bill Cosby smile has been winning friends for Bill since he was a school boy.

When Bill graduated from elementary school, his favorite teacher took him aside. "You're a very intelligent young man," the teacher said, "but you should be working at it."

Bill didn't understand what his teacher meant. "I refused to accept the responsibility to do well in school," he says. "I don't know what I had in mind. It wasn't that I was going to be a professional football or basketball player, or an artist or a drummer; it's just that I wanted to play. I played my whole youth, and every day I'm sorry for it." Still, Bill tried hard to please his mother. He knows that her good example kept him out of trouble.

Glossary

This glossary gives an explanation of how certain words were used in this book. A definition of each word can be found in a dictionary.

acceptance   belonging to the group.

alert   quick to learn.

appreciated   knew the good of.

athlete   person who is good at sports.

audience   group of people who watch and listen.

borrowed   took money from another person and plans to return it.

classmates   students in his class.

comedy routine   show of funny jokes or stories.

crate   wooden box.

develop   work at, become.

discovered   found for the first time.

district   an area.

eldest   oldest.

encore   additional number in a show.

energy   strength, ability to get things done.

eviction signs   signs saying they must leave their home.

exhausted   very tired.

failed in life   did everything wrong, had no success.

fond   liked.

hauling   carrying.

housing project   group of houses or apartments for low-income people.

humor   making people laugh.

image   picture or idea of a person.

intelligent   smart.

jazz   a type of music.

mess steward   ship's officer in charge of food and dining room.

minister   person who leads in a church.

moving down the economic ladder   became poorer.

neighborhood   area in city where people live.

outstanding   best.

penniless   without money.

pistol   a handgun.

receiving welfare   were getting money from the government.

refused   said no to.

responsibility   duty.

scrawny   skinny.

self-taught   taught himself.

shame   feeling bad.

spin a tale   tell a story.

turned me around   made me think and do the right things.

unselfish   did not think about herself.

vanished   gone, disappeared.

whole youth   the entire time between being a child and an adult.

CHAPTER 3
Goofing Off

In junior high school, Bill stood out as an athlete. He was captain of the tumbling team and played basketball and baseball in the local leagues. Bill also was getting quite a reputation as the class cutup. His grades weren't very good. Bill did just enough to get by. When he entered Germantown High School, he was not a top student.

Because of Bill's athletic ability, he was offered a chance to transfer to Central High School. At that time, Central High was one of the top ten high schools in the country. Ninety-five percent of the school's graduates went on to college. Bill transferred to Central High, but his grades didn't improve. He was on the student council and did very well on the school's sports teams. He was quite popular with the students, but his interest wasn't in his books. He failed nearly every one of his classes and had to repeat tenth grade. Bill transferred back to Germantown High School.

"In high school, I never studied or cared about school," Bill says. "The biggest thing for me was

The first TV variety program for kids was brought about by Bill's interest in young people.

being able to throw a football. I was captain of the track and football teams. I knew I had a high IQ, but I coasted until the tenth grade. Then all of a sudden, I couldn't get by, so I was kept there for two years. I found that making people laugh was one way of getting attention, so I concentrated on that. But it cost me a lot. I would have been 21 if I'd stayed on to graduate from high school. I decided to drop out and join the Navy.

"My mother didn't want me to drop out, especially when she was told by the school that I was a very bright boy. She asked, logically enough, 'If he's so bright, then why isn't he doing well in school?' And the school said, 'Well, his interests are someplace else.'

"I knew my parents never understood what I was about. I wasn't interested in anything except playing ball. I could always read, that was one of my greatest pleasures. But to memorize something that had no feeling, like numbers or theories, didn't interest me at all."

Bill decided to become a medical corpsman (pronounced 'core-man') because, as he jokes, "I read the Geneva Convention, and it says you can't shoot a medic. And we medics were very popular. The first thing the wounded guys in the field would shout was, 'Medic!' "

Bill never saw combat. He was trained as a physical therapist. Bill was stationed in Newfoundland, Argentina, and Cuba, as well as at the Bethesda Naval Hospital in Maryland. He also turned out for track and competed in several track meets for Navy teams, setting a few track records.

It wasn't too long before Bill realized the Navy wasn't for him. "Until the time I joined the Navy, people told me that I was a very bright person and that I should be a lawyer or a doctor. I was really afraid to do those things because it meant lots of work. But the Navy made me get up at 3 a.m. and stand and watch the clothesline, with no clothes on the line at all. When I found out how much

I hated that, I had to re-examine what I should do with my life.

"Now, the only way you can get out of a situation like that is to get yourself an education. You don't want to go back to civilian life and wait on tables; you wouldn't even wait on tables—but just take the glasses off. I knew that was where I was headed. So I decided to become something and use the intelligence I was born with.

"I met a lot of guys I knew didn't have as much upstairs as I did, yet they were struggling to get an education. I finally realized that I was committing a sin, a *mental* sin, so I applied for the high school correspondence program and got my diploma. I went to the base commander and thanked him for what the Navy had done for me and told him I was now ready to go to college. I changed from an underachiever. I realized I had to go out and earn it. That's when you start going forward."

Bill is a fine athlete, but he may have been in a little over his head when he played with the great Harlem Globetrotters.

Glossary

This glossary gives an explanation of how certain words were used in this book. A definition of each word can be found in a dictionary.

attention people watching and listening.

bright smart.

captain leader.

civilian life life outside the army, navy, or air force.

coasted went slowly, didn't try.

combat fighting.

committing a sin doing something wrong.

competed tried to win.

concentrated worked only on one thing.

correspondence program learning by mail.

cost me caused me to lose.

cutup funny person.

diploma paper given by school for finishing studies.

education learning.

get by barely pass.

interests what he likes.

IQ level of intelligence.

local leagues groups of sports teams in the area.

logically making sense.

medical corpsman member of the medical team.

memorize learn by heart.

physical therapist person who helps people move.

pleasures   enjoyments.

re-examine   look again at.

realized   understood.

reputation   what most people thought of him.

situation   place in life you are in.

struggling   working hard at.

student council   group of student leaders.

track records   best scores.

trained   learned what to do.

transfer   change schools.

underachiever   person who does less than he is able to.

upstairs   in the brain.

CHAPTER 4
Show Business

Bill already had done some groundwork toward getting into Temple University in Philadelphia. While competing for the Navy track team in a meet with Villanova University, Bill had been introduced to Gavin White, Temple's track coach. Bill asked Coach White if it might be possible for him to attend Temple on an athletic scholarship when he got out of the Navy, and the coach promised to look into it. Eventually, the details were worked out, and Bill was off to college.

At Temple, Bill enrolled as a physical education major, hoping to become a gym coach. He did plenty to earn his athletic scholarship. Bill threw the discus and javelin, broad jumped, high jumped, and ran the 220-yard low hurdles for Temple's track team. He also played right halfback on the school's football team and tried out for the basketball team. Athletically, Bill did very well, winning the Middle Atlantic Conference's high jump championship with a leap of six feet, and running the 100-yard dash in 10.2 seconds. But

When Bill was voted into the Temple University Hall of Fame, he was presented with a painting of himself as a college football star.

more important, his grades were good. He made the dean's list, which made his mother very proud. Bill felt pretty good about it, too.

"At that point, I knew there was no going back," Bill says. "If I didn't make good at Temple, I knew that a lifetime as a busboy or factory hand waited for me. I made myself do well. On an evening when all I wanted to do was go out with the boys, the fear of what might happen to me reared up, and boom! I was right back in my room studying." For the first time in Bill's life, sports were second to studying.

Yet Bill couldn't keep from clowning around. The other students nicknamed him 'Bogart' because of his dramatic antics on the basketball court. And, of course, there were always the jokes and stories. "Laughter always meant that people liked you," Bill explains. "It was a way to gain acceptance; so I told stories in school, in the Navy, in college, at parties, everywhere I could. They broke people up. People kept asking me why I didn't do it professionally, so I did!"

Bill started telling jokes for money while he was at Temple. "In the summer of 1962, between my sophomore and junior years, I decided to do something crazy," he says. A friend of Bill's owned a small nightclub called The Underground. He offered Bill $5 a night plus tips to tend bar and tell jokes to the customers. The club employed a comedian who sometimes failed to show up. When that happened, Bill was happy to take the stage and tell his stories. The crowds loved it too. Soon, word of the funny bartender spread through the neighborhood. The Cellar, a club next door to The Underground, offered Bill $12.50 a night to work as a stand-up comic.

By studying other comedians he admired, such as Mel Brooks, Carl Reiner, Jonathan Winters, Lenny Bruce, and Bob Newhart, Bill began to polish his comedy act. He found work at other Philadelphia nightclubs and began to get jobs outside of the city. The Gaslight Cafe in New York City gave him a free room and paid him $60 a week to perform there, where he sometimes opened for Woody Allen. Bill managed to keep up his studies at Temple and work at the Gaslight. Soon he was earning up to $175 a week. Then came a chance to perform at the Gate of Horn in Chicago for $200 a week, and a chance to play Philadelphia's Town Hall for $250 a night. Bill couldn't do that and stay on the Temple football team. It was time to make a big decision.

Bill knew that he had great talent as a comedian, and he was getting better all the time. But he knew that if he chose comedy, he'd lose his athletic scholarship, and that would mean leaving Temple University. Bill knew how important college was, both to himself and his mother. But he decided to take a shot at show business. "I don't know how I could have taken such a chance," he says. "But I was making as much as $300 on weekends. Even though I wasn't sure how long it would last, I was determined to see it out.'' In November 1962, Bill dropped out of Temple University.

Anna Cosby couldn't believe it. ''When Bill quit college, I was so unhappy it made me ill,'' she says. ''For six weeks I walked back and forth, from room to room, asking myself, 'Why? Why?' When you haven't finished school yourself and your child turns down a chance for a college degree, it's a terrible experience.''

Bill knew the chance he was taking, but he believed he was going to come out on top. His career grew steadily. Bill performed at the top comedy clubs, one after another: Washington, D.C.'s Shadows and the Shoreham Hotel; the Fifth Peg in Toronto, Canada; the hungry i in San Francisco; Las Vegas's Flamingo; Mr. Kelly's in Chicago; and the Bitter End and Basin Street East in New York City.

People were getting to know Bill on the comedy circuit. Many people helped him out at first. One was Clarence Hood, owner of the Gaslight Cafe. ''He believed in me when no one else did,'' Bill says. ''He looked after me and encouraged me to hope, without a thought of what I could do for him in return.'' Bill got to know other club owners, and comedians George Carlin, Richard Pryor, and Sandy Baron became his friends.

Bill met two other people who were to change his life. One was Roy Silver, who later became his manager. The other was Camille Hanks, his future wife.

Because of his great talent and personal charm, Bill was a successful entertainer as a young man.

Glossary

This glossary gives an explanation of how certain words were used in this book. A definition of each word can be found in a dictionary.

admired   had respect for.

athletic scholarship   money given to someone in sports to go to school.

bartender   person who pours drinks.

broke people up   made people laugh.

clowning around   acting funny.

come out on top   be successful.

comedian   a person who tells jokes and funny stories.

comedy circuit   tour of clubs that showed comedians.

competing   trying to win.

customers   persons who pay.

dean's list   list of the school's best students.

decision   choice of what to do.

details   small matters.

determined   decided.

dramatic antics   pretending to be an actor.

encouraged   urged.

groundwork   work done before.

introduced   made known to.

manager   person who is in charge of Bill's work.

nightclub   place where people go for entertainment.

no going back   felt it was his last chance.

offered gave.

opened started the show.

perform give a show.

polish make it better.

proud felt good about what he did.

reared up came up.

steadily gradually.

take a shot try.

take the stage go on stage.

talent natural ability.

terrible experience some awful thing that happens to you.

top best.

CHAPTER **5**

Rising Star Falls In Love

Roy Silver was a Bill Cosby fan. He worked in a New York City office that managed entertainers, and he wanted to go into business on his own. Roy went to Bill's performances and taped them so that Bill could listen to them later on and improve his comedy routines. He became Bill's manager.

Allan Sherman was a good friend of Roy Silver. Allan also was a comedian who had made several records of funny folk songs. He quickly became a Bill Cosby fan, too. In late 1963, Allan was asked to be the guest host on *The Johnny Carson Show.* He invited Bill to appear as a guest on one of the shows. Bill was a big hit. Before long, Bill was invited to be on the *Garry Moore Show,* the *Jack Parr Show,* and *Hootenanny.*

In 1963, Warner Brothers released the first Bill Cosby comedy album, titled *Bill Cosby Is A Very Funny Fellow . . . Right!,* which was recorded live at New York's Bitter End. The album was produced by Roy Silver and Allan Sherman. Bill's first album was a big hit. It went as high as number 21 on the record charts and was in the top 100 for 128 weeks. So Warner Brothers came out with another comedy album by Bill, called *I Started Out As A Child,* which was recorded live at Mr. Kelly's in Chicago. It, too, was produced by Roy Silver and Allan Sherman, and like the first album, it was a big success with more than $1 million in sales. Bill began to work at the Flamingo Hotel in Las Vegas, Nevada, and at Harrah's Club in Lake Tahoe, Nevada. He even performed at the special request of President Lyndon B. Johnson. Less than two years after working for $5 a night, Bill was receiving $1,500 and more a night for comedy shows. The ball was definitely rolling.

In addition to Bill's talent, his success was due to the fact that he was in love. He'd met Camille Hanks in 1963, while working at The Shadows in Washington, D.C. Camille, a psychology major at the University of Maryland, was introduced to Bill by mutual friends. "At first, I was asked to go out on a blind date with Bill, but I refused," Camille says. "I wasn't interested in having a blind date, especially with an entertainer. Growing up as I did, I believed everything awful I'd ever heard about show business people, and I was afraid. But later, someone brought Bill to my bowling class, and he sat in the back, cutting up as usual. He didn't look at all like the ogre I'd expected, so we went out.

Cosby

During the 1960s, Bill became one of the best-known TV stars in America.

"I thought he was a very funny man. Afterwards, he sat in the car and talked all about himself, what he wanted to do about his future and everything. He had a great personality and was a lot of fun. He impressed me with his sincerity and humor."

The following weekend, Bill asked Camille out on another date. Then he surprised her by asking her to marry him. "I was quite shocked," Camille says. "We hadn't known each other long at all." She told Bill that she needed some time to think it over and get to know him better.

Bill carried on a long-distance courtship with Camille. He was working at The Bitter End in New York City, where he would finish his act at three or four in the morning, sleep until 9 a.m. or so, then drive 200 miles to Maryland to take Camille out on dates. Sometimes Bill would be so tired that he'd fall asleep at the movies. "That's when I fell in love with him," Camille says. Three months after Bill proposed, she said "Yes."

Camille's parents were less than thrilled. Her father was a research chemist at Walter Reed Hospital, and her mother ran a nursery school. They wanted their daughter to have a good, secure marriage, and Bill was not their top candidate. "They hadn't realized that we were so serious," Camille says. "The main thing my father objected to was my quitting school. My mother acted just like a mother. She just didn't want me to get married. I was 19, and Bill was 26. They saw him as just a fast-talking comic who wanted to take their daughter away, and they didn't like the idea of my being whisked away like that."

Bill went to Silver Spring, Maryland, to meet the Hanks family. "On that first visit, I was making $450 a week, and when I went back a second time, I was making $750 a week. Camille's mother was suspicious about that. She didn't see how I could be making so much money. Anyway, she didn't want an entertainer running off with her daughter."

The Hanks sent Camille to stay with relatives in Virginia to get her away from Bill, but eventually they gave up and agreed to the marriage. Bill and Camille were married on January 25, 1964, in Olney, Maryland.

The newlyweds' honeymoon was predictable. Bill was booked at the Basin Street East in New York City on his wedding night. Camille traveled with Bill as he toured the comedy circuit. "I had to get used to being with a lot of people," she says. "I lost the privacy I had known all my life. I also had to get used to entertaining and smiling and being gracious. This is natural with Bill. He's much more outgoing than I am. He just loves people, period."

True, but Bill loved Camille more than anyone else. He was anxious to find a home where they could settle down. That wasn't possible until Bill got a part in the TV series *I Spy*.

*Bill's first TV acting job was in the series **I Spy**. At first, he didn't know what he was doing, but he became so good he won Emmy awards as the best actor in a TV series for three straight years.*

Glossary

This glossary gives an explanation of how certain words were used in this book. A definition of each word can be found in a dictionary.

anxious   wanted badly.

ball was rolling   his career was really growing.

blind date   date between two people who do not know each other.

booked   had a job.

business   work on his own.

comedian   a person who tells jokes and funny stories.

cutting up   making people laugh.

entertainers   people who delight or amuse other people.

fan   person who likes Bill Cosby.

folk songs   songs of common, working people.

gracious   showing good manners and being kind.

guest host   person who is filling in for the regular star of the show.

honeymoon   trip after the wedding.

impressed   gave a strong feeling.

less than thrilled   not very happy.

long-distance courtship   he tried to win her love though he lived far away.

mutual friends   friends they both had.

natural   comes easily.

newlyweds   people married a short time.

objected to   was against.

ogre monster.

outgoing friendly.

personality what type of person he was.

predictable knew what would happen.

privacy being alone.

proposed asked her to marry him.

psychology major she studied the mind and how people act.

recorded live recorded in a nightclub—not in a studio.

refused said no to.

released given to stores for the first time.

routines shows.

secure safe.

settle down make a home.

several many.

shocked surprised.

sincerity he was true and honest.

special request he had asked for him in particular.

success did well.

suspicious had lots of questions.

top candidate best person to marry their daughter.

toured traveled to many places.

whisked moved away quickly.

CHAPTER **6**

TV Fame And Fatherhood

Bill's appearance on the *Tonight Show* led to his being chosen for the *I Spy* TV series. One of the millions of people who saw the show was Sheldon Thomas, a TV producer who had worked on *The Dick Van Dyke Show* and several other TV hits. Sheldon, who had once been an actor himself, thought Bill might be great in a part he was creating for the coming *I Spy* series. Sheldon gave Bill a screen test, and Bill got the part of Alexander Scott on *I Spy.*

Robert Culp, who played the part of Kelly Robinson, was Bill's co-star on the show. Robert was an experienced actor; Bill was scared stiff. When everyone got together to begin filming the first episode, Bill found it hard to act. "I was so bad that I was an embarrassment even to myself," Bill says. "The word came down from the executives: 'Get rid of Cosby!' But Bob told them that if they fired me, they'd have to fire him too. He asked for a little time to work with me.

Bill and Camille accept his award for best actor in a TV series in 1966.

"Bob and I got together and talked, and, at Bob's suggestion, we agreed to make the relationship between our two characters, Kelly and Alex, a *beautiful* relationship based on friendship; that way people could see what it would be like if two cats like that could get along.

"When I started on *I Spy*, it was obvious I was a terrible actor. Put me on a stage before a live audience of 5,000 and I was cool, man. But in front of a camera, I'd freeze. I didn't even know how to walk so it looked right. I think it was months before we shot a scene that Bob didn't have to tell me what to do and how to do it. 'Hold the gun this way,' he'd say. 'Face the camera when you bend down. React to this line.' There was just no end to it. Bob was doing two full-time jobs: playing his part and coaching me in mine. I'd be nowhere if it weren't for him. He was very unselfish and a tremendous help. After about the seventh episode, I felt I could walk into my part. It was almost as if I just woke up one morning, went to work, and it was *cool*."

I Spy was a smash success. Bill won the Emmy Award for being the Best Actor in a Dramatic TV Series for three years in a row. By the time the series ended in 1969, Bill was a very big star. His family was rapidly growing, too. Camille and Bill had found a 25-room house in Beverly Hills, and by 1969, Bill was the father of three children.

First came Erika Renee Cosby, the first of four daughters. Bill was so convinced that Erika would be a boy that he prepared an ad for *Variety* magazine that read, 'I got the first man for my softball team.' After Erika was born, Bill ran the ad anyway, with a line that read, 'Oops!' But Bill wasn't disappointed at all. He threw himself into fatherhood, spending as much time as he could with his daughter.

Next came a second daughter, Erinn Chalene Cosby. Erinn was born a few weeks early, and Bill stayed by Camille's side, nearly missing a comedy appearance in Denver, Colorado. Bill spent even more time with his family than before, and his wife and daughters often traveled with him.

Then, in 1969, came Ennis William Cosby, a son. Bill wanted to call him William Henry Cosby III, but Camille was against it. "All right," Bill said, "I'll name him Harry!" That didn't please Camille, either. Finally, they settled on the name Ennis.

"By the way," Camille asked Bill after they had made up their minds, "how *did* we decide on the name Ennis?"

"I don't know," Bill admitted. "But I am completely satisfied with the choice. Now each kid's name begins with E—for *excellent.*"

The Cosbys used that formula when they named their next two daughters, Ensa Camille Cosby, born in 1973, and Evin Harrah Cosby, born in 1976.

Bill loves being a parent. "Camille and I are strong parents," he says. "Once we say something, we mean it. We let our children try a large variety of things, and we let them make decisions. But, at the same time, Camille and I are not reluctant to dictate to our kids in areas where we feel we're the experts.

"We consider our children's schoolwork to be very important," Bill continues. "We're aware of their progress or lack of it, and we know right away from their teachers whether or not they should be putting in more time on a particular subject. We feel it's our duty not only to love, feed, and clothe our children, but to be on top of whatever they're doing. They know what they *want*, but as parents, Camille and I know what they *need*.

"You know, when I first became a parent, I had certain ideas about how I was going to control the children, and it all boiled down to this: children just need love."

Yes, Bill's home life was happy. Maybe that's why his career was doing so well. As the '60s drew to a close, Bill was a bigger star than ever.

*Erinn and Erika Cosby and their famous dad were fea-tured in the 1983 Father's Day section of **Harper's Bazaar** magazine.*

Glossary

This glossary gives an explanation of how certain words were used in this book. A definition of each word can be found in a dictionary.

appearance   being on TV.

boiled down   said simply.

coaching   teaching.

consider   think of.

control   have power over.

convinced   was sure of.

cool   everything was OK.

creating   making.

dictate   tell them what to do.

disappointed   sad.

duty   job, responsibility.

embarrassment   shame.

episode   part of a long story.

executives   people in charge of the TV show.

experienced actor   he had acted many times before.

fatherhood   being a father.

freeze   not move.

friendship   being friends.

obvious   showed easily.

particular   certain.

rapidly   very quickly.

react   act because of what was said.

relationship   belonging to each other.

reluctant   holding back.

satisfied   felt good about.
scared stiff   very afraid.
scene   a part of the TV show.
settled   agreed.
smash success   it did very well.
suggestion   his idea of what to do.
threw himself into   made a big effort.
tremendous   very big.
two cats   two people.
variety   number of different kinds.

CHAPTER 7
Polishing The Act

While he was earning Emmy Awards for his TV acting, Bill also was busy earning Grammy Awards for his comedy albums. In 1965, his third album, *Why Is There Air?* was released. It went to number 19 on the record charts. The fourth album, *Wonderfulness,* rose to number 7 in 1966. In 1967, Bill released a fifth album, *Revenge,* which made it to number two. He also made two rhythm and blues albums in 1967, *Silverthroat* and *Hooray For The Salvation Army Band,* and one of his songs, *Little Old Man,* became a pop hit for two months. Bill also helped produce an album for the Watts 103rd Street Rhythm Band during that year.

In 1968, Bill's sixth comedy album was released. Titled *To Russell, My Brother, Whom I Slept With,* the album rose to the number 7 spot. Like the five albums before it, the album won a Grammy Award. In fact, Bill won the Grammy Award for Best Comedy Album six years in a row, from 1964 to 1969. No other comedian has ever done that.

By the end of the 60s, Bill had one of the biggest collections of Emmy and Grammy awards in all of show business.

There have been many more Bill Cosby comedy albums. Some are *It's True! It's True!; When I Was A Kid; 200 MPH; My Father Confused Me; What Shall I Do, What Shall I Do; Inside The Mind;* and *Bill Cosby Is Not Himself These Days, Rat Own, Rat Own, Rat Own.*

Bill loves music, particularly jazz, but he doesn't really consider himself a musician. "It's just a hobby," he says, "like some guys enjoy golf." In fact, Bill's style of comedy is based on jazz. "I structure my comedy the same way jazz musicians work. To me, a joke is a tune that has a beginning, a middle, and an end. I'm the soloist, and my chord changes are the punch lines that make people laugh.

"I use what I call a 'free form' method. I have a mental outline of what I'm going to do, but I actually work it out while I'm onstage. I have to sense what to do from the audience. If something works well, I'll make a mental note to polish it and use it again. This is the best way for me, because I really trust the people. The important thing is that I *feel* funny. Everybody has moods, but an entertainer can't afford them in his public life.

"I feel that in-person contact with people is the most important thing in comedy. While I'm up on stage, I can actually put myself into the audience and adjust my pace and timing to them. Only through this total communication can I really achieve what I'm trying to do. My humor is based on real-life situations."

Bill's theory of comedy certainly worked for him. As he polished his performance on stage and on records, his TV work continued. "I started with *Sesame Street* three weeks after it went on the air," Bill says with pride, "and from there I went to *The Electric Company.*" He also appeared in several special educational TV shows for children. Meanwhile, *The First Bill Cosby Special* appeared on TV in 1968, followed by a second special in 1969 and a third in 1970.

After *I Spy* was canceled, Bill didn't have to wait long for another spot on TV. *The Bill Cosby Show* was the top-ranked new show of the 1969 TV season, with Bill playing the part of Chet Kincaid, a lovable high school P.E. teacher. That show stayed on the air until the spring of 1971.

By this time, Bill was ready for his next project. Titled *Fat Albert and The Cosby Kids,* the project was a cartoon show based on characters Bill had made famous through his comedy routines. Bill was anxious to produce a TV show that would teach proper values and behavior to the kids who watched it. He set up a special panel of teachers to advise him, headed by Gordon L. Berry, an assistant dean at the University of California at Los Angeles. Bill introduced each show and appeared again at the end. He loved working on the shows. "I can be silly," he said. "I can be a grownup. I can be an older brother. I can be just a funny man that the kids know.''

Fat Albert was a big success. Six million kids were tuning in every Saturday morning. The show won several awards, and Bill was very pleased. He began to work on yet another TV series, *The New Bill Cosby Show*, which went on the air in 1972. This variety show was up against tough competition, *Monday Night Football*, and lasted only one season.

Bill tried one more series for NBC. He waited until 1976 to do it. This show was titled *Cos*, and even Bill knew it had problems and might be a flop. ''My first series, *I Spy*, ran three years,'' he said. ''*The Bill Cosby Show* lasted two years. My first variety show lasted one year. And *Cos* ? If I'm lucky, it will run 13 weeks.''

That's what happened. But Bill wasn't worried. He knew that he'd try again and that the winning formula just hadn't been found yet. ''I just haven't been able to put together the kind of show that will make the public say, 'Hey, let's watch!' '' he said at the time. ''It's as simple as that.''

But Bill wasn't lacking for things to do to keep himself busy. He was working on something that he'd put off for a long time . . . his college degree.

After I Spy, *Bill became the star of his own successful TV series,* The Bill Cosby Show. *It was the top-ranked new show in 1969.*

Glossary

This glossary gives an explanation of how certain words were used in this book. A definition of each word can be found in a dictionary.

achieve   gain.

advise   give ideas on what should be done.

anxious   wanted badly.

audience   group of people who watch and listen.

behavior   way to act.

can't afford them   would lose too much.

cancelled   stopped.

cartoon   a funny show with drawings—like a comic strip.

characters   people in the show.

comedy albums   records of his jokes and funny stories.

communication   talking between Cosby and his listeners.

consider   think of.

earning   deserving to win because of hard work.

flop   show that fails.

hobby   something a person does for fun.

jazz   a type of music.

lovable   someone you could love.

moods   feeling happy or sad.

musician   person who plays an instrument.

outline   list showing main points and sub-points.

pace   how fast he tells jokes.

panel   group of people gathered to talk about ideas.

particularly   especially.

pleased   happy.

polish   make it better.

pride   feeling good about it.

proper value   good ideas on what is right and wrong.

public life   life away from home.

punch lines   words that end a joke.

put off   did not finish.

real-life situations   things that really can happen in life.

released   given to stores for the first time.

sense   feel.

soloist   person playing an instrument by himself.

special educational   learning for students with special needs.

structure   put together.

style   the way he tells jokes and stories.

theory   ideas that tell why.

top-ranked   best liked.

tune   song.

variety show   show with singing, dancing, acting, and comedy.

went on the air   was shown on TV.

winning formula   the way to make a hit show.

CHAPTER **8**

Laughing While You're Learning

Bill was in a position to try school once again. He was making good money both as a TV star and a stand-up comic. Bill was asking $50,000 a night for an appearance and getting it. Bill also had a good income from his records, advertisements, and commercials.

So he decided to do something that people who drop out of school rarely do: go back. "After I performed at the University of Massachusetts once in the late '60s, I started thinking about it," Bill says. "I met with Dean Dwight Allen, who told me I should give it a shot." Bill wasn't content with going back just for a bachelor's degree. He wanted to get his master's and doctorate as well. To do that, he would have to complete his undergraduate work at Temple University.

So that's what Bill did. Temple gave him credit for classes he took at the University of Massachusetts, as well as for his practical experience. Bill received a bachelor's degree from Temple's School of Communications, and he enrolled in a graduate program at the University of Massachusetts.

The Cosby family moved to Amherst, Massachusetts, so Bill could more easily attend school. The family settled into an old 15-room mansion on 286 acres of land and busily redecorated and furnished the house.

Bill graduated in 1977 with a doctor of education degree. It probably was the proudest moment of his life. His family and friends were there to cheer him on. "If Mom were dead, she would have gotten up to come," says Bill. "She always told me that education is a must. Her tears made it all worthwhile."

His 242-page doctoral dissertation was on a familiar subject: *An Integration of the Visual Media via Fat Albert and the Cosby Kids into the Elementary School Curriculum as a Teaching Aid and Vehicle to Achieve Increased Learning.* In other words, how to use Fat Albert and the Cosby Kids on TV to help elementary school kids learn in the classroom. Bill earned his doctorate for the work he was doing with his cartoon show and other educational film projects.

"When I was going to school in the '50s," Bill said, "George Orwell's book *1984* with the infamous 'Big Brother' taught us to fear any sort of screen that talked to us. But somewhere along the way, I realized that television could be programmed to work with children who want to learn. And that's what I try to do with *Fat Albert:*

Bill created the Fat Albert cartoon show to help kids learn while watching TV.

combine learning with entertainment on commercial television to reach 30 or 40 million people, and not all of them kids.

"Achieving an education and going further in school is something that I wanted to do for myself. But I also wanted to show my children that human beings can do three or four things at one time, and that you can accomplish many things in life beyond what you do for a living. I wanted to show them that things are not all that hard, as long as someone is there to explain it to you, and that we should not be afraid of those things."

Bill believes that children can learn and be entertained at the same time. "There's no harm in laughing while you're learning," he says. "That's the key to the way I teach. Teaching kids and providing a good example for them is very important and meaningful to me. I love being around them, and I feel I gain as much from them as they hopefully learn from me. I am a lucky man."

Bill continued to work in TV, including making ads. It was easy for Bill because he endorsed only products he liked. "When the Coca-Cola Company first proposed that I make a commercial for them in 1969," Bill says, "I thought, 'These people are going to *pay* me to say that I love to drink this, when it's what I love to drink *anyway*?' And then came the Jell-O Pudding ads. Why, my mama used to make that for our dessert!"

Bill began to work in films, too. His first movie, *Man And Boy,* was released in 1972. It was a western, and Bill was the star. The film wasn't a big box office hit, but it was profitable.

More films followed. *Hickey And Boggs,* also released in 1972, starred Bill and his former *I Spy* partner, Robert Culp. Then came two films co-starring Bill and Sidney Portier, *Uptown Saturday Night* in 1974 and *Let's Do It Again* in 1975. Next

Sidney Poitier was Bill's costar in the film comedy **Let's Do It Again.**

was *Mother, Jugs & Speed* in 1976, co-starring Bill, Larry Hagman, Raquel Welch, and Harvey Keitel.

A Piece Of The Action in 1977, again with Sidney Portier, was next. Then came Bill's most successful film, *California Suite* in 1978, starring Bill, Richard Pryor, and many other actors. One interesting thing about *California Suite* was that Bill played the part of a doctor, a role that he was to play again with great success on his next TV series.

Glossary

This glossary gives an explanation of how certain words were used in this book. A definition of each word can be found in a dictionary.

accomplish do.

achieving gaining.

advertisements notices in newspapers or magazines to sell a product.

appearance doing a show.

attend to go.

box office hit movie that makes a lot of money.

commercial short film to sell something.

commercial television television paid for by the selling of products.

complete finish.

content satisfied.

doctoral dissertation special paper written for his degree.

educational film films that teach.

endorsed products gave his support to sell things.

enrolled became a member.

familiar something he knew a lot about.

former from his past.

furnished put furniture in.

good income enough money to live on.

key important idea.

mansion very large house.

no harm nothing wrong.

position   place or time in life.

practical experience   what he had done in his work.

profitable   made money.

programmed   made to have a plan.

proposed   asked.

proudest moment   felt very good about himself.

received   was given.

redecorated   made the house more beautiful.

undergraduate   studies of a college student who has not gotten a degree yet.

worthwhile   important enough to do it.

CHAPTER **9**

The Cosby Show

Sometime around 1980, Bill began to develop an idea for a new TV series. He decided to work on this project after he got a satellite dish to improve the TV reception at the Cosby's Massachusetts home. "We could get 25 stations, and the kids loved it," Bill says. "But we created a new problem. It was no longer that the kids were watching too much television. Instead, we had to monitor the type of shows they watched.

"If not monitored, my kids could watch four different movies showing cars smashing, people getting drunk, and sex and violence.

"I grew up loving television. To me, it was a wonderful, magical invention. Television is a fantastic medium that could very well be something, and *should* be something, a family can look at and enjoy. It should *not* be something that we feel afraid to turn on because it will grossly offend us or do a disservice to our children."

Bill decided to create a show that entire families could enjoy together. "It was cheaper to do

In the early planning for **The Cosby Show,** *which went on the air in 1984, Bill thought he would play the part of a chauffeur. Camille, his wife, told him no one would believe it.*

a series than to throw out my family's TV sets,"
he jokes. "I felt that we should go back to the
basics. I wanted to show a family like the kind I
know, with children who are almost a pain in the
neck, and parents who aren't far behind. A husband and wife who have their moments of love
and smiles, yet who sometimes don't really like
each other." Bill wanted to show a family that was
very real.

Two TV networks, ABC and CBS, turned down
Bill's idea. But NBC liked the idea and ordered
at least seven shows for the 1984 season. Bill and
Camille worked together to create the characters.
At first, Bill wanted the father and mother to be
a chauffeur and a carpenter, but Camille was
against that. "Bill," she told him, "nobody is going
to believe that you're a chauffeur. Your image has
always been Temple University, college, and grad
school. Nobody's going to believe it when you put
on a uniform and stand beside a car and start
polishing it. And people are going to laugh in your
face when they see your wife with a hammer."

Bill got the message. He decided to make Cliff
Huxtable, the father, an obstetrician, and Clair,
his wife, an attorney. The network went along
with the idea. Bill and his associates went to work
on the show. The theme song for *The Cosby Show,*
titled *Rastatherian,* was co-written by Bill and
composer-arranger Stu Gardner. Bill helped write
the scripts and helped produce the shows. And he
hand-picked the other actors in the cast.

Phylicia Ayers-Allen got the part of Clair. "There were three finalists for that part, and Phylicia won flat out," Bill says. "She knew how to look at a kid and say, 'You go upstairs to your *room*,' and the kid knows that if he doesn't do it, he's going to find himself walking on hot coals without his shoes. Phylicia was able to say, 'Case closed!' with just her *eyes!*

"Lisa Bonet, who plays the part of Denise, also was an obvious winner. She was just what I wanted—a fashion- conscious teenager who is hip but appears to be a little off-center and might just decide to be Greta Garbo. She's not on drugs and isn't supposed to look like she is, but I wanted Denise Huxtable to seem a little spaced-out, and Lisa has that quality.

"Theo, the son, was tough to cast. There were three finalists, and all had a similar way of reacting to the parent telling them to do something. They sucked their teeth and rolled their eyes before answering. I said the same thing to all three, separately: 'Would you act like that with your father?' They all said they wouldn't. So I asked them to talk to me the way they would talk to their fathers. When Malcolm Jamal-Warner came back, I loved what he did. The moves were right; he was talking to his *dad*. He's a very flexible young actor.

"At that point, I knew that there were going to be four kids in the Huxtable household, and I wasn't too sure that I wanted one of them to be

The Huxtable family members are played by (top row left to right) Tempest Bledsoe, Malcolm Jamal-Warner, Lisa Bonet, (middle row) Bill Cosby, Phylicia Ayers-Allen, and the youngest member Keshia Knight Pulliam. The oldest daughter, played by Sabrina LeBeauf, is not pictured here.

a six-year-old girl. But when I met Keshia Knight Pulliam, I said, 'OK, she's very, very bright, and she'll be able to handle it.' " Keshia became Rudy on the show.

"What's funny is that in the beginning, we all agreed that the Huxtables would have four children," Bill continues. "We left out the character of my real daughter Erika, who was away at college. It wasn't until after we did the first show that I felt my oldest daughter was missing; I really wanted her to be part of that family, in terms of my ideas. Sondra Huxtable, who's played by Sabrina LeBeauf, a very fine actress, is now our oldest girl. You see, in terms of having that family work, I *needed* an older daughter away at college."

The Cosby Show was a tremendous success, reaching the number-one spot its first season. "I'm pleasantly surprised at the show's success," Bill says. "I was just hoping it could stay on, because I have so much to give. The show is really a love story to people. It's about what I studied at the university; it's about my gratitude that I finally woke up as a youngster and went to college; and it's about my love for telling and writing stories. Most of all, though, it's entertainment for the whole family."

Bill is so concerned about the messages sent to the viewers who watch *The Cosby Show* that he has asked Dr. Alvin Poussaint, a psychiatrist at the Harvard Medical School, to look at the scripts and make suggestions. "My one rule is to be true rather than funny," Bill says. "Family and kids are what I know best. It's an extension of my real life. You have to understand that the real success for this show comes from the fact that my life reflects the lives of so many other human beings."

Glossary

This glossary gives an explanation of how certain words were used in this book. A definition of each word can be found in a dictionary.

associates   people he worked with making the show.

attorney   lawyer.

carpenter   person who works with wood to build a house.

characters   people in the show.

chauffeur   person whose job is to drive a car.

created   made.

develop   work on.

disservice   bad action.

entertainment   something that delights or amuses people.

entire   whole.

extension   added part.

fashion-conscious   likes clothes.

flat out   without question.

flexible   able to change.

gratitude   being thankful.

grossly offend   cause you to be very mad.

hip   knows the latest.

magical invention   something made that seems unreal.

medium   way to give ideas.

message   what she had to say.

monitor   watch over.

moves   his actions.

networks   major TV companies.

obstetrician   doctor who helps women with having babies.

obvious   easy to see.

pleasantly   happily.

psychiatrist   doctor who treats mental illness.

quality   something about her.

reception   the sharpness of a TV picture.

reflects   shows the picture of.

satellite dish   large, round object for receiving TV signals from space.

scripts   written stories.

season   part of the year.

separately   by themselves.

spaced-out   doesn't know what is going on.

suggestions   ideas of what to do.

theme song   show's song.

tremendous   very big.

walking on hot coals   in trouble.

CHAPTER 10
"A Smile On My Face"

Bill Cosby knows that he's come a long way. The funny little kid from the Philadelphia housing project who was the class clown has grown up into a well-educated, serious professional entertainer. Bill feels that sooner or later he would have become an entertainer. "I think that no matter what career I would have chosen, medicine, law, or teaching, I would have gone into performing," he says.

Bill is good at what he does, and he knows it. "If I were a youngster wanting to study stand-up comedy," Bill says, "I'd study me!" Not many people would argue with Bill on that point. "This isn't conceit," he says. "It's just that I know what I can do, and I also know that by doing things the way I want to do them, people will support me."

For Bill, love is what it's all about. "When you go on stage, you're embarrassed to come right out and say, 'Love me,' but that's really what you're doing," he points out. And people have come to love Bill, and his TV family. "I believe that the

"If I were a youngster wanting to study stand-up comedy, I'd study me."

main reason our show is being watched all across the country is because everybody is saying, 'You know, I have a kid who acts exactly like that,' " Bill says. "Our show brings people together. For me, this series is a love affair for all the years that I've been a well-paid entertainer. It's my way of saying to the people who have enjoyed my work, 'I can do this, and here is a form of entertainment that I hope you will all feel good about.'

"I want to put a show on the air that people can be proud of and identify with, and, most importantly, a show where children can laugh at the behavior of parents and parents can laugh at the behavior of children.

"I feel as though the love I have to give people is appreciated. I tell you, I get sort of silly with happiness when I think about it, and I just want to give more and more and more. Usually, I hardly ever watch my own work, but with *The Cosby Show*, it's different. I watch every week. And at the end of every segment, I find myself with a smile on my face, because I really like that family and the feeling they give me."

Of course, Bill saves the bulk of his love for his wife and children. "I love Camille more and more as I grow older," Bill says. "That lady has stood so solidly with me for all these years. Whenever the time comes when one of us needs the other's support, that support is there, and it's real because we love each other."

How does Bill show his love for his children and make them understand that he's concerned about them? "It's very difficult, and I've relied on the values of the old days," he says. "Every one of our children can testify that I told them, 'There will be none of this!' at times. I let them know that

Bill teaches kids, "Whatever you do, put your whole self into it."

I love them, but that we expect respect within the family.

"I tell them that I'm going to leave them an awful lot of money, but that nobody is getting anything unless they have a formal education and can understand what to do with that money. I tell them what Sophie Tucker said a long time ago: 'I've been poor and I've been rich, and rich is better.' "

There is nothing more important than being a parent, Bill believes. "The most important educational vehicle in life is a parent figure," he says. "We need more involvement from parents; they must realize that deep down, most children want somebody to tell them how to go. Perhaps if we can get children to love and respect their parents, they'll want to please them. And if we can get children to have love and respect for their parents, perhaps they'll do the turnaround themselves."

Bill believes that you have to try as hard as you can to do your best. He remembers how he almost quit acting when he first began his TV career on *I Spy.* "At first, I was afraid to put 100 percent effort into acting," he says. "But that kind of fear is a trap. The more you find you can do, the more you find out about yourself.

"If there were just one lesson I could leave to my kids, it would be this: whatever you do put your whole self into it. So few people really give all of themselves to anything because they're afraid to. But once you discover you're capable of succeeding at things you thought you didn't dare try, you find you can do even more."

Glossary

This glossary gives an explanation of how certain words were used in this book. A definition of each word can be found in a dictionary.

appreciated thankful for.

behavior way they act.

bulk main part.

capable able to do.

conceit thinking too much of himself.

concerned worried.

deep down true feelings.

difficult hard to do.

embarrassed feeling badly.

entertainment something that delights or amuses people.

expect something he wants strongly.

form kind.

formal education finish studies at school.

housing project group of houses or apartments for low-income people.

identify with see themselves.

involvement parents being part of a child's life.

100 percent all.

parent figure father or mother.

put your whole self try your very best.

realize understand.

relied depended.

respect children and parents to show honor to each other.

segment   each show.
serious   thinks about what is important.
solidly   strongly.
support   be behind him.
trap   something that catches animals or people.
turnaround   make them do what is right.
vehicle   something that carries people or things.
youngster   young person.